The Philosophy
of Paul Watson

FRANK JOHNSON

CONTENTS

INTRODUCTION

Paul Watson is one of the best known environmental activists in the world today. Very instrumental in the early formation of Greenpeace, he has devoted his life to helping protect the environment and in particular animals of the sea.

One cannot fail to respect Watson to the major powers he has stood against in his mission to save the sea life (particularly whales), standing up to the likes of Japan and despite his non-violent protests has even spent time in jail for his devotion to his causes.

However, Watson remains a very controversial character, appearing to lack sympathy for the people of Japan following the 2011 earthquake and even being labelled a terrorist by some.

Much quoted in the media, Watson has used this presence to promote his ideology for a world in which greater controls on fishing are essential.

This book brings together some of his most notable quotes, about a variety of subject including himself, animals and politics.

ABOUT HIMSELF

"I do what I do because it is the right thing to do. I am a warrior, and it is the way of the warrior to fight superior odds."

*

"I wouldn't think I was successful if I didn't have just as many people hate me as support me."

*

"I did not establish the Sea Shepherd Conservation Society as a protest organisation."

*

"I would just say that nobody could do what I do unless you had a big ego. It's the only way you can really put it. You have to be arrogant enough to challenge the arrogance of the human race."

*

"I used to swim with these beavers in a beaver pond when I was 10. I went back when I was 11 and found there were no more beavers. I found that trappers had taken them all, so I became quite angry, and that winter I began to walk the trap lines and free animals from the traps and destroy the traps."

*

"I don't care if I put people off."

*

"There are many who condemn my crew and I for taking the law into our own hands and for taking on the barons of corporate profit."

*

"When I was born, there were three billion people on the planet."

*

"Nobody has ever been hurt by the actions of ships I have been on."

*

"I have an unexplainable belief that I will never cause harm or be harmed while at sea. Because of this, I feel secure at sea: I feel secure in the ice, I feel secure in the storms, and I feel secure in confrontations."

*

"People say I manipulate the media. Well, duh. We live in a media culture, so why on earth wouldn't I?"

*

"I don't have a religion, but I respect them."

*

"I take a biocentric point of view. I look at things from the point of view of the Earth and the laws of ecology. As opposed to the anthropocentric point of view, where everything revolves around humanity."

*

"I've won some awards. 'Time' magazine designated me as one of the environmental heroes of the 20th century. Oh, and I've got some honorary citizenships, like from the Conch Republic of the Florida Keys. But the one thing I am proud of is I didn't get the Chevron environmental award. Never did get that one."

*

"Being lampooned on 'South Park' is hardly something to complain about. They brought the issue of the dolphin and whale slaughter by the Japanese to a very large audience. I could not really care less how I was portrayed."

*

"I'm not interested in culture; I'm interested in the law."

*

"My grandfather carried me around on his shoulders at 85."

*

"In 1993, I chased Cuban and Spanish drag trawlers off the Grand Banks off of Newfoundland. And it cost them $35 million in losses."

*

"The Brer Rabbit ploy has been quite effective for me. When a country is talking about prosecuting me, I demand to be charged and put on trial and offer to pay my own airfare. They know that I'm going to bring a lot of international media with me and put their whaling programme on trial, and they decide it's better to keep quiet and do nothing."

*

"I always try to take the unexpected things and make them work for me."

*

"I always say, 'I'm not a pirate, I just play one on TV.'"

*

"I was doing a talk show in Vancouver, and somebody called in a bomb threat to protest my violence, which I thought was pretty strange. We had to evacuate."

*

"I'm thankful to have time to write."

*

"I'm not pessimistic about anything."

*

"I'm not really a fugitive."

*

"I'm never horrible to anybody. My problem, and you can ask any of my friends, is that I'm too nice to everybody."

*

"Actually, I never really look at myself as a real radical activist; I am more the conservative. I mean, the conservatives are trying to conserve; the radicals are destroying the planet."

*

"No words can describe the personal liberation that heading seaward bestows upon me. In this aquatic realm, no man or woman is subject to the petty decrees of social bureaucracy."

ABOUT OTHER PEOPLE

"I have known Farley Mowat all of my life, from reading his books as a child to becoming a close friend of his over the last three decades."

*

"Captain Falco saw the diminishment of biodiversity in our oceans over a span of nearly seven decades. He was dedicated to the protection of life and habitats in the sea. He was a legendary mariner, diver, oceanographer, and conservationist. The world is a better place because of him."

*

"Pete Bethune is a hero in New Zealand. He's a hero worldwide to people who want to see the end of whaling."

*

"Way back in October 2007, I had urged thousands of Australians to vote for Kevin Rudd and Peter Garrett's Labor Party. Why? Because they promised to get tough on illegal Japanese whaling."

*

"I have actually led more expeditions to Antarctica than Scott, Amundsen, and Shackleton put together."

ABOUT PLANTS AND ANIMALS

"I feel that we have a responsibility to try to do everything we can to protect species, and the best way to do that is to uphold international conservation law."

*

"I have never suffered under any delusion that saving the whales in the Antarctic sanctuary would be easy, but the one thing I am certain of is that I and my passionate crew of international volunteers will never quit defending life in the seas from poachers, no matter what consequences we must endure to do so."

*

"There's money to be made by driving a species extinct."

*

"Sustainable fishing is a fraud. It's a marketing term that really means 'business as usual.'"

*

"The sealing industry is dying."

*

"Domestic house cats kill more fish than all the world's seals put together."

*

"The shark is the apex predator in the sea. Sharks have molded evolution for 450 million years. All fish species that are prey to the sharks have had their behavior, their speed, their camouflage, their defense mechanisms molded by the shark."

*

"I find it abhorrent to see a whale being slaughtered
and do nothing but bear witness."

*

"Whales are killed today to supply the limited demand
for whale meat or to be used in pet foods or as fodder
for fur-bearing animals used in the fur trade."

*

"Killing a baby seal is about the easiest thing you can
do if you're inclined to be sadistic; you certainly can't
say there's any sport in it - the animal is totally
defenceless."

*

"An American citizen is not going to be extradited to
Japan for saving whales."

*

"Bluefin tuna is sort of like the cheetah of the ocean. It's the fastest fish. It's a warm-blooded fish. But it's got a $100,000 price tag on its head."

*

"People sometimes feel frustrated about what's going on in our oceans and environment, and 'Whale Wars' shows that ordinary people can take action and make things happen."

*

"I don't eat fish because there is no such thing as sustainable fishing in the world right now."

*

"A fish is more valuable swimming in the sea maintaining the integrity of oceanic eco-systems than it is on anyone's plate."

*

"Ships are expendable; the whales are not."

*

"I have been honoured to serve the whales, dolphins, seals - and all the other creatures on this Earth. Their beauty, intelligence, strength, and spirit have inspired me."

*

"The Polynesians used to have a system where they proclaimed a fishing area as 'taboo.' If any fisherman was caught fishing in a taboo area, they would be killed. The Polynesians understand that the fish had to be given a chance to recover."

*

"If we wipe out the fish, the oceans are going to die. If the oceans die, we die. We can't live on this planet with a dead ocean."

*

"Every fish in the ocean is in danger."

*

"No species is more important than others."

*

"To me extremism is targeting endangered whales in a whale sanctuary in violation of a moratorium. That, to me, is extreme."

*

"We'll lose more species of plants and animals between 2000 and 2065 than we've lost in the last 65 million years. If we don't find answers to these problems, we're gonna be victims of this extinction event that we're at fault for."

*

"The biggest predator of fish like cod is other fish - and seals keep fish like that in check."

*

"As long as there is a Southern Ocean whale sanctuary, Sea Shepherd crew will continue to patrol and defend it."

*

"The Sea Shepherd Conservation Society recognizes that the deaths of four sealers is a tragedy, but Sea Shepherd also recognizes that the slaughter of hundreds of thousands of seal pups is an even greater tragedy."

*

"I don't see the point in making a distinction between natives having more of a right to kill whales than nonnative people."

*

"In 'Deadliest Catch,' we have men in ships in rough seas catching crabs. With 'Whale Wars,' we have men and women from a dozen different nations going out to sea in rough weather to help save the whales. We also have icebergs, whales, penguins, and dramatic ship-to-ship confrontations."

*

"My clients are the whales and the seals."

GENERAL PHILOSOPHY

"It's a war, I think, to save the planet, really, from
ourselves."

*

"I don't think you really have to retire from what you
do."

*

"You will not ever perceive the truth that is reality.
There are many realities."

*

21

"All confrontation is based on deception."

*

"We buy a bottle of water in the city, where clean water comes out in its taps. You know, back in 1965, if someone said to the average person, 'You know in thirty years you are going to buy water in plastic bottles and pay more for that water than for gasoline?' Everybody would look at you like you're completely out of your mind."

*

"All revolutions are violent revolutions."

*

"Protesting against illegal activity is not piracy."

*

"There's no rest when you're on planetary duty."

*

"Protesting is fundamentally submissive."

*

"The oceans are the last free place on the planet."

*

"We're close to losing our essential diversity. Look at our wheat crops - we rely on a handful of grain crops and plants that we've refined and bred over hundreds of years."

*

"You don't get anywhere unless you've had a little bit of a complicated life."

*

"The most powerful weapon in the world, as far as I'm concerned, is the camera."

*

"Follow your dreams and use your natural-born talents and skills to make this a better world for tomorrow."

GREENPEACE

"I will not watch a whale die. I've not seen a whale die
since I left Greenpeace in 1977."

*

"There are quite a few disgruntled Greenpeacers who
are opposed to its policy of non-cooperation."

*

"Greenpeace is the world's largest feel-good
organisation now, and I can say that 'cause I am one
of their co-founders."

*

"Greenpeace has a fast ship that could stop the whalers cold."

*

"People feel good about giving money to Greenpeace."

*

"Does Greenpeace think it can stop whaling in Antarctica by publicly eating whale meat and declaring it delicious? What are these people thinking?"

ON COUNTRIES

"Dutch prisons are probably the most civilized you're going to find anywhere in the world."

*

"The film 'The Cove' made people aware of the Japanese slaughter of whales."

*

"In Ecuador, if I go after an Ecuadoran, I'm in trouble; if I go after a Costa Rican, I'm a hero."

*

"My concern is not for the judicial system, but for the reality that the shark fin mafia of Costa Rica has a price on my head, and a Costa Rican prison would provide an excellent opportunity for someone to exercise this lethal contract against me."

*

"The Sea Shepherd crew is doing what governments should be doing, but refuse to do themselves, because of the threats of trade retaliation from Japan."

*

"Canada I don't trust. The Canadian government hates me more than the Japanese."

*

"The fact is, Japan's whaling is illegal, so just because there is a natural disaster in Japan is no reason for us to stop opposing their illegal activities in the Southern Ocean."

*

"Taiwan gives a lot of foreign aid to Costa Rica, so it looks like they are basically buying the right to fish, even though it's not legal."

*

"The seal hunt has made me ashamed to be a Canadian."

*

"Russian subs are a bargain at $60,000. Unfortunately, none of the dials or instructions are in English."

*

"Costa Rica and Germany have simply been pawns in the Japanese quest to silence Sea Shepherd in an attempt to stop our annual opposition of their illegal whaling activities."

*

"The only language that the Japanese whaling industry

understands is economics."

*

"Japan is a bully nation that takes what it wants and threatens any who oppose it."

*

"I want to stay in the ocean. I'm not going to be able to do that from some holding cell in Japan."

*

"In Africa, the rangers shoot poachers."

ON PEOPLE

"Social change comes through people."

*

"I feel that people should have a license to have children, that they have proper education how to raise children. And that nobody should be allowed to be a parent unless they can prove that they are competent enough to be a parent."

*

"We live on the most incredible planet, and yet we abuse it, and we abuse it mercilessly."

*

"We need to stop flying, stop driving cars and jetting around on marine recreational vehicles."

*

"Everybody is a hypocrite. You can't live on this planet without being a hypocrite."

*

"That's the thing with celebrities: the media can't ignore them."

*

"People are beginning to realize that we need to live in accordance with the law of ecology, the law of finite resources, and if we don't, we're going to go extinct."

*

"Sometimes we are separated by differences, and sometimes we are united by common ideals of respect and compassion."

POLITICS

"The environmental movement doesn't have many deserters and has a high level of recruitment. Eventually, there will be open war."

*

"In December 2012, the U.S. 9th district court granted a temporary injunction to the Japanese whalers that ordered the Sea Shepherd Conservation Society U.S.A. to not approach within 500 yards of the whaling vessels."

*

"I've had a lot of disappointments. I think my biggest

disappointment is the failure of elected officials to make good on their promises in regards to the environment or anything else, really. I have very little faith in politicians."

*

"I don't think that any government has a right to subvert the truth or to cover up the truth, and all I see WikiLeaks doing is exposing the truth."

*

"Sometimes going to jail is just the price you have to pay for social reform or social change."

*

"Any social movement throughout history has always been carried out by only 7% of population being passionately active in that."

*

"NATO isn't going to be concerned about fishing."

*

"The United Nations World Charter for Nature, section 21, empowers any nongovernmental organisation or individual to uphold international conservation law in areas beyond national jurisdiction and specifically on the high seas."

THOUGHTS & OPINIONS

"Here's the thing: Nobody gets extradited for a crime where nobody's been hurt, where no property's been damaged."

*

"I experienced the California Northridge Earthquake of 1994 and the eruption of Mount St. Helens in 1980, and I have thus seen firsthand how terrible and awesomely devastating a force of nature can be."

*

"Most people can't see the connection between their own lives and the oceans."

*

"If you're dealing with criminals, they're not going to want to go to court."

*

"The only thing scarier than Godzilla is Godzilla's lawyers."

*

"It is true that many of the Sea Shepherd crewmembers are inexperienced, but the fact is that these volunteers bring a passion to the project that cannot be found in a hired crew."

*

"There are very few fishermen left today."

*

"Usually, environmental programs are not designed
for a mainstream audience."

*

"Nobody can legitimately claim to be a marine
ecologist and conservationist while continuing to eat
fish. It is the ultimate form of hypocrisy."

*

"Ecoterrorism is terrorism against the environment."

*

"Immigration is one of the leading contributors to
population growth."

*

"Sea Shepherd does not condone, nor do we practise,
violence."

*

"The tragedy is that there is so much more incentive - money - to destroy the ecology than there is to preserve it."

*

"When I hear so-called professional journalists ask why we have celebrities speak for us and for the animals, the environment or social causes, I marvel at their denial of the rules of their own trade."

*

"Documentaries make a difference."

*

"Spermaceti oil is valued for its high resistance to heat, and thus it is used in machinery where there is excessive heat."

*

"Putting Zodiacs in front of whaling vessels doesn't do it anymore. Done that, been there, seen that."

*

"Sea Shepherd is to terrorism what Groucho was to Marxism."

*

"Commercial fishermen are the greediest, stupidest people on earth."

ALSO BY FRANK JOHNSON

INSIDE THE MIND OF CHUCK PALAHNIUK

THE WIT AND WISDOM OF JOSS WHEDON

INSIDE THE MIND OF EMMA WATSON

THE VERY BEST OF MICHAEL MOORE

Made in the USA
Middletown, DE
23 September 2019